Contours

poems by

Sandra Sturtz Hauss

Finishing Line Press
Georgetown, Kentucky

Contours

Copyright © 2016 by Sandra Sturtz Hauss
ISBN 978-1-944251-72-7 First Edition

All rights reserved under International and Pan-American Copyright Conventions. No part of this book may be reproduced in any manner whatsoever without written permission from the publisher, except in the case of brief quotations embodied in critical articles and reviews.

ACKNOWLEDGMENTS

I would like to thank the following journals for their publication of individual poems:

Oasis 2008 Leila Joiner, Editor (Imago Press) "At the Gazebo in Larchmont"
A Slant of Light Lawrence Carr & Jan Zlotnik Schmidt, Editors (Codhill Press Books) "Downfall"

My poem, "Stages of a Man's Career," is based on the following from the Quote Investigator website:
"The earliest evidence known to QI was printed in the syndicated Hollywood gossip column of Mike Connolly in September 1960. This clever template describing the trajectory of recognition for a celebrity was sent to the columnist by the actor Hugh O'Brian and his name was featured repeatedly: 1
Hugh O'Brian gave me the following points—as The Five Most Important Stages in the Life of an Actor:
(1) "Who is Hugh O'Brian?"
(2) "Get me Hugh O'Brian as the star of our next picture!"
(3) "Get me somebody who's a Hugh O'Brian type."
(4) "Get me a young Hugh O'Brian."
(5) "Who WAS Hugh O'Brian?"

Special thanks to my husband George for patiently listening to and commenting on endless drafts and revision.

I would also like to thank the members of my poetry community, the workshops, classes and roundtables I attend. I feel fortunate to have their friendship and helpful critiques.

Editor: Christen Kincaid

Cover Art: George E. Hauss

Author Photo: George E. Hauss

Cover Design: Elizabeth Maines

Printed in the USA on acid-free paper.
Order online: www.finishinglinepress.com
also available on amazon.com

Author inquiries and mail orders:
Finishing Line Press
P. O. Box 1626
Georgetown, Kentucky 40324
U. S. A.

Table of Contents

Lincoln Center 1
Change of Heart 2
At the Gazebo in Larchmont 3
Pan 4
Wonderment 5
Ordinary Day in the 50's 6
Celluloid Fragments 7
Choreography, Girls 9
Alfred 10
Pas de Deux 11
On Their Tenth 12
Scents of Time 13
Then and Now 14
Incarnations 15
Nightsongs 16
Harry Hilpert 17
Ode to the Electric Chair 18
Carole Lee and the Tiger Lilies 19
In Mourning 20
The People in the Picture 21
Interlude 22
Something Borrowed, Something Blue 23
Helen, In Autumn 24
Downfall 25
Stages of a Man's Career 26
On the 807 27
Metropolitan Symphonies 28
Ephemera 30
Contours 31

*In memory of my grandfather,
David Greenspan, whose love
of writing has been my inspiration*

Lincoln Center

It's what I would miss most,
these Friday nights we share:
married-people chatter
on the drive to the City,
stracciatella gelato
from the concourse kiosk,
hot soup as winter approaches;

how when the lights dim
we run our fingers lightly
along each others' forearms
or just hold hands;
how we scope out first-tier seats,
scramble to them during intermission,
pretend to be latecomers;
how you came to love Mozart's 40th
even more than I.

These nights I become even more
aware of you, your sexy blue eyes,
your cologne. I'd miss the ride home,
me sighing, "I miss the cats," you pretending
you don't, then lying in bed watching old movies.

Change of Heart

After thirty minutes you could smell
the sweetness from anywhere in the
neighborhood; with half-an-hour bake time
left I'd anticipate cutting through those
crunchy flakes, peeling moistened sugar
and cinnamon from the knife, licking

my buttery fingers. Before we had our
consciousness raised: cottage cheese and
sour cream, margarine and egg yolks,
real sugar and vanilla all blended over
a whole pound of broad egg noodles.
I prepared Rose's Noodle Pudding recipe

for every special occasion, so many when
in my youth, when pots shone like mirrors,
before gravy stains set, refused to be scrubbed
away by Ajax or Brillo. Who thought about
cooking healthy? It was the sixties, I was
a young bride and big was always better.

Not like today when two cups sugar convert
to sixteen pink or yellow packets, when
seven eggs become six egg whites and
no one with a conscience uses margarine.
Today's added sweetness comes from a can
of crushed pineapple. Yet, it is still warm

and comforting, smells even more inviting,
wafting through a four-bedroom house
from a huge, ultra-modern, oversized kitchen,
three miles and a lifetime away from that
one-bedroom, one bathroom, one-ten-a-month
on Winchester Avenue.

At the Gazebo in Larchmont

I'm watching a man who reminds me of you,
Whose voice and movements conjure up an image
That makes me wish you were here with me now
So we could sit together and write.
Grandpa, I'm speaking with this man
Whose voice is so like yours
That tears are falling from my eyes
And my own voice becomes inaudible,
So hard is it for me to speak
For memories are flooding my brain
And my heart wants to reach out to him
To be closer to you.
He tells me he sits on this park bench each day,
Just watching the movement and reflecting on life
The way you would if you were still here.
He speaks with an accent so familiar to me
For my childhood was spent hearing that warm inflection,
And his eyes are warm recollecting his love
From a wife now long gone and his children, both living.
He wears a fur coat to be shielded from winter
And sits on a pillow for his bones are now aged,
He walks with a cane though his steps are still steady.
Grandpa, when we spoke, I swear I was with you
And felt it was fate to have met him
Just when I was missing you most.

Pan

Years of encrusted blackness form swirling cloudlike
patterns. Misshapen, wobbling on the burner, it is
a poor man's heirloom with a rich legacy. Awakened
by sweet aromas of creamy melting butter, I danced

into our kitchen, Grandpa scraping *kratsich*, browned
flaky crust, onto perfectly scrambled eggs. I remember
their exotic feathery feel on my tongue. I still hear his
booming voice, *Tschibitshis eggey, Mommy?* Six decades

later, I am sole guardian of that small, sacred skillet. Its handle
is a sturdy bridge to my childhood. *Carry you, Gumpa.* I study
the charred pieces of history, anchor of family fingerprints. The
years are melted onto its uneven surface, never to be scraped clean.

Wonderment

They perch on the windowsill,
mesmerized, like onyx statues,
by softly falling snowflakes,
a ballet in white,
settling on bare branches,
resting on the ground.

Were it not snow
but scurrying squirrels,
their strong feline frames
would thrash about,
leap across my living room,
eyes darting left, right,
tails batting like metronomes.

But snowfalls seduce them,
engage their natural curiosity.
I enter their tranquil world,
embrace the stillness,
muted blues and grays of dusk.
I light the fireplace.

Ordinary Day in the 50's

Eight-year olds with scraped knees
we screech at screened windows,
Throw down a dime for ice cream.
Ding ding, dinging, as he rumbles
down Bolton Street, trades
our tissue-covered coins
for orange ice over vanilla,
creamy chocolate fudgsicles
that drip circular stains
on white polo shirts.
Champion roller skaters,
we careen around our block,
unaware, unafraid.
Sheriffs, we saunter into town,
flash silver badges, loaded pistols,
reclaim The Cliffs before sunset
until sweaty and tired
we empty water guns,
unbuckle holsters,
drift upstairs for dinner.

Celluloid Fragments

Monte Valley
summers '51 '52
Catskill bungalow colony
eight-week respite
from Bronx humidity
mothers occupy large rooms
or small cottages
with the children
husbands form a Bull Train
    drive up Friday
    leave on Sunday

Dad completes
the threading
our lives unfold in eight mm
frame by frame
we relive
wordless summers of eternal youth
and innocence
I splash in sunlit
turquoise, my face a toothless smile
    inflated plastic
    circles my waist

I watch the film
almost smell the chlorine
Mom's eyes follow me everywhere
unaware of men
leering at her
years later she reveals many
in their circle
made advances
on the grass outside the cottage they
        assemble a lounger
        it keeps collapsing

their hilarity
invites a crowd
the final attempt draws applause
viewing this reel
they laugh
like they've never seen it before
the way they did
after hanging a shelf
upside down on newly hung wallpaper
        or when he locked their
        car keys in the trunk

Choreography, Girls

my father said,
Move those arms,
you'll never get famous
just standing still.
Forty years later,
thinking in could-have-beens,
I watch yesterday's doo-wop groups
on late night specials.
Step forward, together,
back, together,
sway slowly sideward,
pivot, pivot, turn.
Arms in unison float
like scarves dancing in midair—
push forward, then again,
tighten fists, slow release.
Voices deep and sensual
cry *Baby,* plead *Come back.*
Four men in powder-blue tuxedos,
three sopranos in pink-sequined satin.
A night of quartets and trios
recalling our era,
when we harmonized
love found, love lost
just standing still.

Alfred

There's a photo
of him as a young boy,
six, maybe seven,
astride a pony.
Same impish face
till the day he dies—
eighty eight, almost eighty nine.

A cherished young boy:
doting mother, ailing father,
dead before the boy's *bar mitzvah*,
leaves an older son to guide him.

The boy in the photo is unaware
his mother will remarry:
Old Man Krantz,
white-haired gent,
deep kindly voice.

The boy doesn't know
his mother will die
in a black woolen overcoat,
day eight of a nine-day heat wave.
He has yet to discover passion,
the lust and love he'll feel
for the Polish beauty
who will someday become my mother.

Pas de Deux

Perfectly partnered,
shyly seductive, she
basked in his devotion
for seven decades.

Recalling a bygone era,
they were Fred and Ginger
in *Apple Blossom Time*.
They moved as one: she
followed his lead, he
devoured her with his eyes.

Migratory birds, they
flew in formation, exuded
grace and sensuality.
Perfect precision,
choreographed to a symphony
only they could hear.

On Their Tenth

She dazzles in deep blue,
a taffeta shirt-waist that swishes
as she dances across our living room.
My father's eyes sparkle
every time she walks by.
Bright red *Hazel Bishop* fires her lips,
Evening in Paris, sensual on neck and wrists.
She is everything I want to be.

I strain to understand the adults' chatter
as they tap their crystal goblets.
With ice floating in my milk and puffing
a paper straw, I wander past couples
I call *Aunt and Uncle So-and-So*, friends
I see when we view our eight millimeters.
The men, ties loosened and *Brylcreem* in their
parted hair, get louder as the evening progresses;
their wives, in Alexander's dresses and pearls,
cluster in groups to compare their lives.

Dad reads his paper,
waits for her to empty ash trays
and half-filled glasses, hand wash her good dishes.
She removes Patti Page and Dean Martin
from the Victrola, changes into her red nylon nightie,
heads upstairs.

Scents of Time

Once a dark-haired beauty,
Evening in Paris on her wrists,
Saturday nights in the City with
my father, his clean-shaven cheek
splashed with Old Spice.

Sunday mornings, tying her floral apron,
she fried bacon and eggs in the charred pan
I'd inherit in five decades.
Afternoons she enticed with home-baked
chocolate cake, freshly-brewed Maxwell House.
On Friday evenings, neighbors caught a whiff
of fried onions, roast chicken, warm buttery biscuits.

Mother's Day, bouquets of fresh lilacs
covered living room tables, newly polished
with Guardsman. Mondays I would accompany
her to the roof, Clorox stinging our noses,
wooden clothespins in our basket.

I remember the leathery scent of our cars,
each year a different model for my salesman Dad.
I remember the smell of wet fur on Spanky and Pudgy,
Charlie cologne on Mom's newer hostess robes.
I try to recapture each now that he is gone
and she has only fleeting images of the past.

Then and Now

Use your walker, I plead.
Oh, she says, I never take it
when I shop with the girls.
How long since she shopped with the girls?
Danced with my father?
Played canasta with neighbors?
Your house is too cold, they complained,
then stopped coming over,
neglected to invite her.

Adele, it's your turn
Adele, what are you doing?

Once so vibrant,
stunning in her simplicity,
the little redhead with a big heart—
seemingly shy till you gave her
a microphone, a cause, an office
to run. She's where you went
for attitude adjustment, rosy-eyed
outlook. Nothing got her down
enough to lament her lot.

She would have, though, when
she lost her soul mate, when their
70-year honeymoon ended. How
fortunate he passed just as
her memory began to fail.

We have to go now, Mom.
Use your walker.

Incarnations

I live as a purple finch
in weedy fields and floodplains,
happiest in winter,
my brilliant scarlet and shiny black
glittering on snow-laden branches.

I fly with bouncy undulating pattern,
call in flight to the ground below, alight
on roadsides of jagged topography to
observe the world of humans.

What have you done to the land?
I sigh, pinching my beak
to keep from trembling.
*You destroy, pollute, encroach; you
make me choke and sputter. Soon
you will miss our avian chorus,
rainbows of cobalt blue,
rose-colored lilac.*

Eons from now,
reborn in human form,
I will return. My song will emerge,
a triumphant hymn
called *Atonement*.

Nightsongs

Sleep eludes me,
symphony of midnight's wakefulness.
His snoring crescendos,
loosely masked by white noise.
A rainstorm manifests
with the press of a button;

a humidifier hums,
sends a steady stream
of lukewarm mist
that settles everywhere.
Music blares from car radios,
teenage drivers propelled by testosterone.

I tiptoe upstairs, my sanctuary,
where pale blue walls
embrace a Victorian landscape.
A purring cat sprawls across my chest.
His pulsing heartbeat relaxes me.
At daylight two more cats

await the flutter of sparrows
nested in our air conditioner.
Cat tails bat like metronomes,
eyes widen, ears perk as they
tumble over each other,
hearken to the sunrise song.

Harry Hilpert

We never met, but
I would have liked you.
You exuded toughness when
we needed strong fighting men.
Rough exterior, gentle soul,
featherweight boxer with a dancer's
stance, dazzling in that 1940's way,
lithe, agile like Fred Astaire,
popular, especially with the ladies.

I married the little boy who rode his bike
up and down those Bronx streets,
who called you Grandpa so long ago.
He has your good looks and generosity,
treasures those rides in your taxi,
remembers how you stepped in
for his absent father, and more than
anything, that you considered him
your favorite.

Ode to the Electric Chair

His is massive.
He propels himself around
their two claustrophobic rooms,

scratches the furniture,
slashes the brown leather futon
where a full-time Jamaican aide sleeps.

He opts for the fastest speed, never
sitting still, spinning, moving in reverse
the way he lived his entire life.

He once stood proud, handsome
and daring, legs strong enough
to support his large frame—

a quarter century ago, when I first
married his son. A self-described
character, he sits tall in his chair,

adjusts to whatever curves life throws,
reaches for Mom's quavering hand,
whispers, *It's okay, Baby, I'm still here.*

Carole Lee and the Tiger Lilies

Five friends,
all in their fifties,
all in straw hats.

We laze in her backyard,
glasses brimming
with sweet lemonade.
Summer stories flow.
Each of us talk over one another.
Each of us check to see she's still awake.

The brilliant orange
of her tiger lilies—
their long stems sway,
absorb the sunlight.
They grow wild like the cancer
consuming her body.

She's happiest in the garden.
A smile peeks out from under
her straw cloche, the one
with shoulder-length synthetic hair.

In Mourning

The buffet table is ready. Our best
dishes, silver, platters await cakes,
fruit, chocolates. Soon the smell of
fresh coffee permeates the air. There
is no party. We are sitting *shiva*.

For seven days we sit on low stools,
unshaven, not allowed to bathe, work, leave.
Torn black ribbons symbolize broken hearts.
Covered mirrors prevent displays of vanity.
Doors unlocked, visitors enter, bearing
sweets, offering words of consolation
we barely hear. Mourners mingle, flit

from sofas to bridge chairs, balance
cups, saucers. It begins:
I'll never forget when we...
It seems like only yesterday...
He was always so...
Laughter, introspective quiet, laughter—
the sounds of bittersweet.
Shared moments, private conversations,
jokes, anecdotes.
We remember.

The week ends.
The deafening silence begins.

The People in the Picture

In life he was hard as yellow jasper,
Rare moments of mirth or laughter.
In photos a softness emerged,
Penetrated the camera lens,
Cut through the morass of sadness
To soften the lines of his anguish.

The rest of us stood beside him,
A parade of silent smiles,
Pretense you find in most photographs:
They capture brief moments when
Lives coalesce, families stand tall,
Arms around one another,
Dignity intact.

For years we tried to pierce the armor,
Find the man in the photo,
Joyful one with passion and playfulness,
The one we didn't need to hide bottles from
Or approach with trepidation.
Only on his deathbed did we discover him,
Small, helpless, yet filled with love,
Addressing God, begging salvation.

Interlude

That summer screeching silence
became the norm, vitriol spewed forth
in staccato whispers; darkness crept
into every corner.

Trembling, we hid behind sofas,
crouched outside their bedroom door,
clung to each other. Too young to
escape, too scared to confront,
we waited.

One crisp morning he washed
Mother's car, raked the leaves
then left. Without a word, he lugged
a large leather suitcase out the front
door, down the stone walkway,
into his Buick.

For weeks teardrops shimmered
on her pale cheeks; she paced
up and down hallways,
one half-smoked cigarette
lighting the next.

Eyes glazed, she shopped for food,
cooked our meals. We went to school,
did our chores, pretended everything was fine.

Just before Thanksgiving he returned,
resumed his place at the table,
said Grace. For years we speculated,
tried to fill in the empty spaces,
but never asked,
never knew.

Something Borrowed, Something Blue

Unlike today's strapless, tightly-fitted dresses,
mine had long sleeves and a full skirt—a ball gown.
We honeymooned in Miami Beach, flew home
one week later to our one-bedroom, one bathroom,
one-hundred-ten-dollar-a-month apartment,
me more excited about being a wife than marrying

this particular man. Yet, there was something
about the smell of newly-laid linoleum, smooth under
my bare feet, how grown up I felt arranging crystal
wine goblets in the china cabinet or hanging flowered
nylon curtains in our freshly-painted kitchen. I filled
a linen closet with matching towels, heavenly soft sheets

to enfold me after a long day in front of a classroom.
In those days, not yet jaded and with little money,
everything said *special*: that first food shopping spree
when seventeen dollars bought a week's groceries,
meat included; the newly-published New York Times
Cookbook with its sturdy blue cover proudly displayed

on my slightly cracked countertop. *Sadie, Sadie,
married lady* cooked, cleaned, laundered, entertained,
had her own Ford Falcon and a full-time job. It was all new
to this twenty-year-old bride who thought we'd grow old
together, then realized after a decade I already felt old
and left.

Helen, in Autumn

No leaves dawdle on Helen's lawn. As they fall
from her majestic oaks, she plunges a death rake
into their golden brown backs, quickly piles and
bags them for pickup. Helen never dances across

her yard, never feels autumn's blanket crunch under
her shoes. In twenty five years since her mom passed,
we've rarely seen visitors—a few retired ladies she
taught with, a man we believe is her brother. Mostly,

Helen parks her Chevy, picks up the mail, climbs
the steps to her front door. We wonder about
the house's interior, if it's pristine like the lawn,
if a lover ever spent the night. Did Helen ever

romp in snow, sled down a hill? It's as if her dreams
rest in that lawn. Once autumn's leaves vanish, Helen
will center a Christmas candle in each window, try
to catch each snowflake before it lands.

Downfall

Lady Jane visited nightly, first chatting
amiably, soon stumbling over words,
by midnight stumbling over the rest of us.
So pretty, slender, a good neighbor,
seemingly respectable, but always one cigarette,
one Screwdriver, one married lover away
from respectability.

Dear Jane, her ash blonde hair
primly pulled back, revealing the lovely
face of a fallen Irish Catholic; she
punctuated stories with props, puffed,
sipped and tittered, smoothed her hair.
Always spilling drinks, then tears, finally
secrets we should never have been privy to.

Lonely Jane, every day a liquid lunch;
suit stained, lips smeared, awaiting
the inevitable pink slip. We can only
wonder how she made her way home,
negotiated the road, the long hallways
leading to her apartment.

Finally sobered, Poor Jane,
after a late-night stumble
found in her bathtub
not in proverbial gin,
but scalding water.

Stages of a Man's Career

A new young actor hit the stage
Who'd not yet paid his dues
'Twas years till he'd become the rage
Folks asked, "Who's this Tom Cruise?

He made more films, became well known
Earned fabulous reviews
Directors hurried to the phone
Yelled, "Get me this Tom Cruise."

Amounts he charged became a factor,
Directors blew a fuse
Studios said, "Send me an actor
Who looks just like Tom Cruise."

So as time passed, still more acclaim
And granting interviews
But now directors would exclaim,
"I want a young Tom Cruise."

As we all know life's so sublime
And someday we all lose
Eventually there comes the time
It's back to, "Who's Tom Cruise?"

On the 807

Hurry, scurry, always moving,
forward, backward, breakneck speed,
rushing, crushing, dashing, crashing,
push me, pull you, yes indeed.

Crowded platforms, leaning over,
waiting, grating railroad's roar,
gotta get there, where ya goin'?
Won't know till they shut the door.

Walking, stalking, whining, pining,
thinking you'll avoid your fate,
Death's appointment in Samarra
does not falter, will not wait.

Damn it, stop and smell the roses,
take a moment, give some slack,
you must realize once it's over
you ain't never comin' back.

Metropolitan Symphonies

They drive in
from quiet suburbs,
board buses in
mid-western towns,
Main Streets where
shop owners call you by name.
They fly here from overseas
converse in German, French, Farsi.
Light-skinned and dark, they
pursue the City's excitement,
seek their images on screens
above a concourse the mayor
closed to traffic.
I see us.   There we are.
as a scarlet sweater or blue cap
distinguishes one from another,
a mountain of unconnected faces
all part of the clatter, the hum of
footsteps that is Broadway—
above the grating roar of subway cars
amidst taxi horns and rolling buses
among seducers who yell, *Comedy
Club tonight, half-price dinners,
tickets to Stomp,* anything to entice.
Costumed characters pose for pay
in souvenir photos. Street musicians
draw crowds, play for loose change.
Hawkers sell gloves, purses, tee shirts.
A lone addict shivers on the street, begs
for sustenance as hardened onlookers
avert their eyes.

An ambulance speeds by, its
wailing siren drowns out voices,
laughter, chiming cell phones.
Crowds look up, look around,
resume conversations,
continue on their way.

Ephemera

Mating calls of light and shadow,
as light bends reality
shadow creates then conceals
kaleidoscopic tunnels,
rainbows of reds.

So many selves.
Naked eyes glimpse naked body
draped in flowing garb,
dancing in daylight
as one becomes two,
become one.

Warrior lovers
assume animal forms,
reside in one being,
hide behind then emerge
from waltzing layers
of white chiffon.

The longer you gaze
the more you perceive
until reality laughs, lingers
just beyond your reach.

Contours

Cold curved marble,
shades of beige
fluid and warm—
a swooping pelican,
bold and hungry,
ballerinas twirling
in ecru tulle,
lustrous seashells
resting in warm sand.

Again I touch
the stark cold object,
invert, move it closer,
then further.
No pelicans or ballerinas,
no seashells.
I ask the others,
What do you see?
They answer: *Beauty. Life. Nature.*
I turn to the artist for guidance.
What is it you want me to see?
There is only silence.

Sandra Sturtz Hauss' work has appeared in journals, magazines and anthologies, on greeting cards, calendars, YouTube and numerous websites. A retired teacher of gifted/talented students, she has facilitated workshops in drama and poetry for children and adults.

Blue Mountain Arts has published many of her inspirational poems in anthologies and on greeting cards; memoir pieces appear in *Good Old Days* and *Looking Back* Magazines. An autobiographical booklet, *The 60's:Times of Change*, was released by Benchmark Education Company. Her work is in journals, including *Oasis 2008, Cyclamens and Swords, Up Against the Wall, Mother* and the prize-winning *A Slant of Light*; she presented original poetry in performance at the Ridgefield Theater Barn. A poetic essay, set to music by Jon Schmidt, can be found on YouTube as "Tranquility – Sandra Hauss."

A Phi Beta Kappa graduate of Hunter College, Ms. Hauss holds a masters degree from the College of New Rochelle. Recipient of an Educator of Excellence award, she taught for 29 years, fostering a love of literature and writing in her elementary school students. As part of the volunteer Poetry Caravan, she gives readings in hospitals and assisted living facilities throughout Westchester. Ms. Hauss attends ekphrastic poetry workshops, writing roundtables and a poetry study group. Her passions are theater, music and animal welfare. She lives with her supportive husband George and their three cherished cats.